REFLECTIONS OF SPONTANEOUS DEEP EXPRESSIONS

GROUP CAPTAIN P K AGNIHOTRI

BlueRose ONE.com DIY
Stories Matter
New Delhi • London

REFLECTIONS OF SPONTANEOUS DEEP EXPRESSIONS

Author: Group Captain Pradeep Kumar Agnihotri
411 AFNO Enclave, Sector-7, Plot -11,
Dwarka, New Delhi-110075 INDIA
9891153445 & 9625973445
Mail Id pradipagnihotri1952@gmail.com

ISBN :978-93-6452-896-2
Web design: Ms Priyasha Agnihotri

Edition: First edition 2024

Price: INR 370/-, 20 US Dollars & equivalent

Publishers: M/s Blue Rose Publishers
Noida (U.P), Kolkata, London

BlueRoseONE.com DIY
Stories Matter
NewDelhi • London

S. No.	Contents	Page No.

FOREWORD

It gives me an immense pleasure to pen a few lines as a foreword to the third Poetry book by **Group Captain P K Agnihotri.**

Pradeep has always been a poet at heart through his long years in the Air Force as a Logistics officer. Although he wrote even while in service, Poetry, his first love, got greater attention from him as a Veteran.

Pradeep has always written about Social issues. Yet, he has also dealt with subjects like Flight Safety with same subtlety as Women Empowerment, Labourer's plight, Terrorism, Spirituality & Romance.

Without having to know much about Poetry, it's structures, writing patterns and formats, the reader enjoys his writing. Rhyming or Free verse, English or Hindi, Urdu Sher-o-Shayari, "Deep" takes the readers along.

This third book promises to complement the two earlier publications titled **"Spontaneity"** and **"Deep Reflections".**

Here **Pradeep** has dealt with a wide range of issues in this **"Reflections of Spontaneous Deep Expressions",** including Pandemic, Tributes to Galwan Valley Warriors. I am sure, it will be a fascinating read.

I wish **Pradeep**, all success and happiness in presenting his Poetry collections to readers

Air Marshal P V Athawale
PVSM, AVSM, VSM,

AUTHOR'S MIND SCREEN

Transition from IAF Sojourn, as a Logistician, to realms of Corporate World, remaining in exclusive domains of creative writings has been indeed a rewarding experience.

It has enriched my aspirations with positive responses and accolades, during my prideful Poetic journey. Same has been boosting my mission, with positive catalyst inputs to enhance my zeal and enthuse me to continue emoting & give shapes in the form of Poetry books.

This resulted in meeting this special prideful destination with the Publication of third Poetry Book "Reflections of Spontaneous Deep Reflections".

It is a matter great honour and glory, my Poetry compilation is being released by distinguished personality of the country, in the presence of illustrious guests of honour.

Group Captain P. K. Agnihotri

DEEP GRATITUDE

With the publication and release of collection of Poetry in English, I am filled with ecstasy giving me a sense of achievement and fulfilment of cherished dreams.

My gratitude from the core of my heart, my proud Parents **"Dr Somesh–Kusum" Agnihotri"** for nurturing seeds of creativity. Similar sentiments flow for Loving in Laws **"Dr. Yogendra-Sharmistha Shukla"** for affectionate shower of encouragement after our family's sacred union. Their prayers helped in achieving personal milestone

My heartful sentiments emerge with salutations for my dearest Sister, **Dr Priti Pandey**, caring dear brothers **Dr Prashant** and **Er Prabhat Agnihotri** who have been my strongest pillars in Life sojourn. Deep salutations to each one of them.

Real Anchor of my nucleus family, caring wife **Mrs. Meena Agnihotri,** has provided ever supportive roles in all occasions during our life sojourn.

My cherished dreams of family were fulfilled by my sons **Rachit** & **Wg Cdr Archit Agnihotri,** a Civil Aviator, his graceful wife **Mrs Ankita Agnihotri** and sweet heart grandson Master **Atharv** adding value additions to the entire family.

Special appreciation for my dearest and talented niece **Ms Priyasha Agnihotri** for her immaculate & superb colour web design of the book's colourful covers.

My most sincere gratitude for a superlative foreword by **Air Marshal P V Athawale** PVSM, AVSM, VSM. for his expressions of encouraging appreciation of my creations

Privileged blessings got showered by my Grand Parents Trust "**Rai Bahadur Gauri Shankar-Laxmi Devi Memorial Charitable Trust" Retina Care Hospital Nagpur** and respected parent's Trust **"Dr Som-Kusum Agnihotri Memorial Charitable Trust"**

Special thanks to **Group Captain Shailendra Mohan** for his expert guidance in giving final shape to the book

Lastly, personal thanks to relatives, Friends, Poets & IAF colleagues who supported me, besides avid readers for their sincere encouragements.

"Deep Regards"

World Of

"Deep Expressions"

SPACE MISSION

Traversed steadily, cruised to blue sky vision
Merged with distant sights of the blue horizon.

Imaginations of colours cast inspirations & delight
Indelible impression of Space journeys so bright

Research mission on Technical domains
Mind medulla of country's space mission.

Showered glimpse of poise & floating attire
Proud countrymen elated & offered prayer

Flashback of a delightful earthly contour
Blissful fruits of endurance & the calibre

Chariot of spacecraft reached blue climax
Crossing barriers of gravity, courage index

On board Soyuz – Apr 1984
Wing Commander Rakesh Sharma Ashok Chakra.
Deep gratitude on behalf of every Countrymen

MOTHERLY TOUCH

Blessed hands garner love link of umbilical thread.
Plasma cells grew bonds of blood in heart & head

Shared vision & wisdom for life goal on ground
Instant guide in dark hours for smiles unbound

Yearn to seek blessings till eternity & beyond.
Bright hopes & lovely harmonious background.

Deep in love, enliven our spirit to rekindle
Desire to live in your arms, playful cradle.

Adore your role of omnipresent friend, a guide
Words fall short for expressions of my gratitude,

Bow to yeoman role to make us part & parcel.

'Deep' Cord

MISSING YOU PAA

Scared to revisit the teary sight of lost part
Remind moments, of love as you depart
Thoughts, on board mental plane, fell apart
Shattered hopes turbulent ocean of torn heart.

Shock wave torment, molten eyes, subdue mind
Cycle down lanes of fond wish, life line entwined
Distant trails envision dark ways, without light
Radiant memories treasure apparently out of my sight.

Blurred vision caused real life myopic aberration
Mind shifted from tranquillity to turbulent ocean
Played role of an anchor, deep sea of prudence
Existence now devoid of meaning to life, in silence

Siphon out hopes, cause strains of stress chains
We remained tensed, impending those last remains
Sojourn, in timed boats, away from of crashed ship
Pull time wheel cart, under memorable era flagship.

Cast an indelible imprint of serene laughter & smiles
End of mystic aura, far away, spread over miles
Warmth of love route, blessed enlightened mind
Ashore sea of loneliness, frequent thoughts remind

'Deep' respectful remembrances

SHRADAHA SABURI

Tensions caused ripples to fathom
Obscured paths led to dark unknown lanes
Across world of realities, beyond the faith zone
Hopes sublimated in fleeting moments of sojourn

Bouts of fearful thoughts shattered mental solitude
Carried sentiments to isolation, of scary magnitude
Sought "SAI" blessings with patience & gratitude
To boost morale strength and fortitude altitude

Distant sky screen brought instant bliss images
Established 'His' presence, as prayers engages.
Powers of invocation proved faith in Almighty's light
Rekindling hopes within heart by an eternal delight

Glow shared faithful praises with admiration
Shradha-Saburi on life ways, Deep expression

In 'deep' Reverence

"Om Sai"

DEEP GRATITUDES – GURU

On rising levels of consciousness,
Invest in pure wisdom, only to bloom
Do ensure your inner purification
Now bedecked, with a rising moon

Radiating true visions of kind gestures
Multitude of rising sun, often discover
Mellow human ego, raises on self-pride
Merge impressions of lifetime shelter

Shower compassion with passionate mind
To protect humanity, with grace & poise
Seek sacred blessings of Guru's divinity
For shower of wisdom petals & advice

Inspire triumph on virtuous path sojourn
Radiate ambience of cosmic innovation
Motivate to bow our heads in reverence
Celestial sounds echo, for minds to churn

Bring abundance in spiritual fortunes
Elevate fortitude & life's joy quotient
Reassure positivity on path of humanity
Bliss of salvation, in eternal mode, so ambient

Deep salutes

RELATIVITY OF LIFE SOJOURN

Memories would always make strides
On our minds, to encircle Head sphere
Heart would always murmur to emote
Relished for long, belong to wish share

Faith would always enlighten our route
Seek blessings on life ways, to travel ashore
Hopes would always ride on parting thoughts
Our shadows can never emulate to care

Thoughts would always eliviate sufferings
Negate barriers of expressions, by blessing share
Obeisance would always augment life meaning
Our life will cease to exist, without deep prayers

Mission to accomplish their life dreams
Would grant heart beats, tow bliss layers
Yearn and would always bow to the spirit
Present in silent prayers, voices so dear

Tears would always troll, taking a toll
On cheeks that can't control and steer

Sublimed Deep faces in Eternity

"ATHARV" A GRAND BOND

Thrives heart vibrations of our world, from start
Shares reflections on our mutual deep love part
Allures with smart sights of twinkles in eye art
Enjoys circling around love spheres

Blessed with innocent smiles attraction
Our heart throb and mind's close affection
Charms ripples are adorable with passion
Pulls us back on lanes of yesteryears

Spreads hands backward, makes a flyers sight
We enjoy his cute expressions, with a delight
Showers his innumerable style in our twilight
Pleasurable actor in sight

Expressive eyes of a cute angel
Patron's care shower from an angle
Tiny bud blooms in our family garden's pales
Divinity flows to fathom affection

Rekindle joy candles within cool hope nest
To boost mind & rise on roof top for a rest
Unbound affectionate love, bestows a crest
Our tender love affair

Grand Atharv bond deep eternal source of love

NISARG- THE DESTINY HIGHTIDES

Standing alone on a thought's boat
Amidst gushing windy forest's blast
Broke monotony of silent coaster
Marred aspirations & lurking disaster

Struck blow on country's western fronts.
Causing flutters on cascading wave fonts
Imagination on turbulent on sea tides
Balance fulcrum on mission's rough sides

Distress on ship waved only stress & strains
Cross hurdles enroute strand of constraints
Built shelter & an eternal guide, faith pride
Anchor thoughts, on merging destiny hightide

Journey with straight strong stems
Tryst as the destiny way's streams
Bring ecstasy moments, in heart domain
Charms of minutes, share hour's delight

'Deep' in Turbulence

Disaster scenes of 'Nisarg' cyclone.

IF ONE COULD

If one could live with disdain
When it is too polluted to exist
If one could cross the terrain
When it is too uncertain to check the depth

If one could ingrain to refrain
When it is too disgraceful to face
If one could avoid strain
When it is too confusing a place

If one could entrain a life wheeler
When it is too fragile to board
If one could curb mind's villain
When he is too novice to understand

If one could be his own captain
When it is too diplomatic to command
If one could chain own thought
When it is too difficult to hold trot

If one could entertain own company
When it is too tough a bargain
If one could train to discipline
When it is too arduous marathon

One would achieve deep goals of life
Even if it is too dependent on destiny

PARTING 'ATAL' WAYS

People gazing at sky, teary eyes
Dark clouds, on political arena and cries

Thoughts took spin, gyrated ponder
Hopes caught behind, For a surrender

Cast images of loss of a true leader of class
Faith tumbles, tear roll down on hour glass

Vanishing sights, as pyre flame spreads
Merge inspirations to emote, on his poetic traits

Tribute poured from compassionate mind
Sought blessings, an ideal leader, so kind

'Deep' Tributes

For Ex PM Shri Atal Bihari Bajpai,

GALVANISING MISSION

With pride of valour encounter & sacrifices
Across line of control safety zones, heavy prices.

Moving vision of bravery, bleeding veins,
Strike with power on targets, ignoring lifelines.

Adorning medals for galvanizing mountain valleys
Great warriors of country borders ward off non allays.

Emotions ride on deep prayer transmission
Emerged silhouette on enemy territory seek attention.
Nation bows with gratitude and expressions
Venting fire & fury, on enemy's deceptive aggression.

Deep Galvanising Mission

MAJDOOR MAYHEM

As the mighty show them doors
Sights of downtrodden pour
Moved by deep despair ashore

Walking on roadside try to discover
Ways of destiny wheels reverse gear
As the mighty show them doors

Dwindling hopes, a tough score
While media strives, only to score
Moved by deep despair ashore

Sights of distraught on road tore
Override on shoulders of loader
As the mighty show them doors

Rhythm of sighs resonate & share
With truncated hopes of life's stairs
Moved by deep despair ashore

Life shifting on support of ventilator
Survive on lost breaths, to endure
Moved by deep despair ashore
As the mighty show them doors

Majboor Deep A Villanelle

WATERY GRAVE – OH ORISSA

Alas, on that dreadful day
Nothing went: right their way
Tranquil serene moments at bay
Broke submerged cries far away

Mere thoughts of giant tidal wave
Merrily march into suicidal grave
Tore imagination's barrier, shook hearts
Agony lasting mere seconds & fell apart

Ghastly scenes of human body's heaps
Merged with soil with short time leaps
Cause repulsions of death replay
Nature's negative role, on painful replay

Marooned Islands of floating body's race
Ripple fear of death, on an ocean cage
Hunger bouts with thirst, on bloated faces
Thrust an end, with unseen last live gaze

Cries within too strong to surround
Deafening waves created loud sound
Calamity's expression power far beyond
Losses of human & cattle lives unbound

Deep watery Grave Impact

SHIV YOG - A WAY OF LIFE

Infusing a divine Energy
Imbibes a role of spiritual guide
Showers blessings to protect
Remove shivyogi darkness aside

Explains difference in knowledge & wisdom
Shares Joy during life sojourn's kingdom
The benign presence of 'Shiva'
An epitome of expression's delight

Avalanche of heartful vibrations,
Thrives on real distinction sight
Inspires to walk on 'Shivyog' virtuous path
Builds faith in life, on enlightened path,

Provides shelter in hope's umbrella
Musters mental strength by love
Serves humanity with radiant smiles
By blissful shower petals for miles

Streams of 'Seva' 'Sadhna' & 'Satsang'
Sun & moon travel in invocation song
Cross mental hurdles & envision
By holding 'HIS' hands in ovation

'Deep' reverence mode & mood.

A RACE DISGRACE

A disgrace to witness failing human race
Unfair trials, on life's ripped apart face
Dismal sights, rode on dark colour of skin
Ripped open humanity & life's value akin

Life surely lost its meaning & existence
Getting trounced by foot merciless intents
Cruel destiny awarded verdict by lawlessness
Executing without trial, merely by unfairness.

Slaughter like a chicken in blocked net
Knifed a black, with their black mindset
Trembling neck gave way to pressure
Losing strength and life too, to endure

Exhibited qualities of black murderer
Endeavoured & stood on till eye's blurred
Cruelty in abundance on offence of pittance
Award death penalty, hung heads in shame

Deep disgraceful atrocity- In a US city

MISSION FLIGHT SAFETY

On entries in to cockpit for flight operations
Wish you relax & follow laid down precautions
Visions of Flight Safety, Avoid "FOD" hills
Fly with precision, raise confidence & skills

Build your will power, on mission of proficiency
Emulate acumen display, for spirit buoyancy
SOP' guided safety mission for glorious flights
Magical sights spread wings, on attaining heights

Yearn for reward to earn, raise the pedestal
With holistic swing, soar spirits on passion trail
Adorn flight safety crest, aim to fly well
Imbibe positive attitude, maintain National will

Build a safety net, on moves in kind
A soft reminder for your soaring mind

Deep Mission Dear Aviator Son

BON VOYAGE

Transit body fence, showbiz admirers
Appalled by grief, on passing away of stars.

Silent lanes of Bollywood stalwarts left apart
Truncated careers of adorable idols in heart

Deep prayers merge on stalwarts move apart.
Lying across fence, swollen eyes, as tears retort.

Pay homages to bright stars, carry a teary train
Mind screen & hurt visions, their part did entertain.

'Deep' silence kept for two minutes for Bollywood stars
Departed with indelible impressions as show stops

Deep Bon voyage

JEEVA-AMRIT

Precious gift of GOD, brought lovely angel.
Blessed bundle of Joy, from a rejoice angle
Cascading labour pain turned pleasure sights
Spectrum of beaming face, bring colours delights.

Parent's love carved to cast dreams into reality
Holding little 'Jeeva' doll with mother empathy.
Fathom charm on Parent's face, now on cloud nine
Promote status of couple to proud joint life line.

Heartful smiles put "Vibhuti" on forehead of emotion.
Playing a sacred role for mutual growth & reunion.
Expanse of world of words, got lovely poetic shape
Tenderness touches epitome, for destiny's reshape.

May the smiles spread for miles over all stations
Enrich every moment, with Joyous unifications
Wish you both enjoy chirping sounds around
Submerge in Jeeva deep love, by pride bond

'Deep' Live wishes

MOVE ON LITTLE DARLING

Embarked on third year, next step of cute adoration
Endorse every soft move with balanced admiration
Spark glows in twinkling eyes, flow of divine love
Cast outbursts of grand celebrations of lovely dove

Blessings shower from atop, with warmth around
No longings for soft toys, your prized gifts on ground.
Your teachers will now yearn, to make you learn
Parent's anxiety would rise, & slog to concern

Deep hopes, for lifetime asset
    You would enter life skill on test.

Always shower bliss acute angels
For protection of His care angles.

"Deep" blessings

UNITED WE FIGHT COVID

Dear Covid Warriors

Look around your personal safety is vital
Serve other's concern, strong covid tidal.
Selfless services with devotion, is matter of pride
Fight relentlessly on grim battles really wide.

We share true empathy to bring broad smiles
Truly concerned on safety & emergent styles
These horrific times of disturbing scenes
Eyes are on you, to save life's essences.

Nature showed utter helplessness side
Wishes for covid override, medical pride.
Your patience adored, & gratitude never hide
Move ahead, we bow our heads, for real sacrifice

'Deep' unity of medical fraternity

MY MINDSET

Wish to gain will for climb to light tower
Wish to maintain trust level in down hour

Wish to sustain & fair function in adversity
Wish to bargain & disarm for nation's unity

Wish to learn from Gurus & spread wisdom
Wish to earn a part of teacher's kingdom

Wish to remain cool, when it's hard to survive
Wish to regain lost hopes to serve and thrive

Wish to spread smiles through my couplets
Wish to imbibe solitude, by thought's droplets

Deep mindset

Yes, Yes, Yes

Age is just a number, don't they say
Shore is just an edge, to cover the bay
One ought to carry own weight around
Withstand pressure & remain on ground

What is in the name carried for so long
Just a way to address amongst few songs
Rustic music lovers rhyme love tunes
Reverberate by heart and swinging tones

Draw closer to earn a clear distinction
Home on to own dwelling destination
Let your beliefs thrive, with broad mind
Care enriches life values, purity refined

Recreate blissful images, in cosy love nest.
Habitat & build dream's land for an invest.
Beauty within, shines effortlessly always
Invocation of mind, refines on pathways.

'Deep' Yes Yes Yes

MEMORY GALLERY

Embarking upon memory celebration sight
Invocation of celestial bliss for divine light
Tons of images appear on mind's blue canopy
Face mirrors to reflect heart & mind's clarity

Wheels of faith move on time track waves
Life continues to take us through rivers & caves.
Emotions thrive on deep self status awareness
Adorable ambience showers trust & fairness.

Smoothen challenge, by deep understanding
Cross barriers and turmoil by power steering.
Merge souls on path of togetherness high spirit
Eternal blessings emerge deep prayers in light.

Deep memory gallery

DEEPLY SHARED WILL

On my departure, wish you sight dark spots
Explore ruined sentiment's heap's isolated stops.

Would discover mingled thoughts, spread in corner
Unbaked emotions beans, on broken lower drawer.

Would find envelope deeply shared will
Open with caution, as emotions may spill.

May see empty Jar lying ajar, in vacuum of hunger
Be resilient, don't run off, due to distress or any fear.

Surely would find dark torn memories on troll
Eyes blanked by lost aspirations orbiting on call

On photo frame hung on wall, will find layers of dust
Its only neglection of my creativity and lost trust.

Don't ransack my world of word stacks wood fire
Make them immortal by positive vibes to inspire

Lifetime treasures and thought pleasures emergence
on mind's screen.

Deep Will shared

MUSE TO AMUSE

People keep pulling other's legs
Though on verge of eminent grave.
Instead should support with shoulders
With clear intents & work like a brave.

Face life's ups & downs in the evening hours
Assist each other without being rave
Stop uncanny attempts to demolish hopes
Built on bricks of porous caves

Restrain review & then entrain
Stop pulling chain without any aim
Print chapters of humanity growth
Resolve to extinguish fire not going in vain

Debar thoughts of space constraints enter open heart
Smoothen love dwelling as your valuable part
Fervent appeals of countries fall on plugged ears
Let not someone try to harm and pain anywhere

Deep amused

GREETINGS DEAR FAUJIS

Fondly rejoice warrior's nostalgic memories
Share brotherly love & affection, treasuries.
Organizational support Nurture serene pride
Glorious years yearned & earned respect, aside.

Life kept flowing with waves of fraternity feeling
Your company kept us in good humour & flourishing.
Milestones of professional domains with distinction
Harmony, friendship & guide kept us with perfection.

Uniform gave reasons for heads a high place to stay
Deep salutes for arduous voyage of professional way.
We stand in ovation, enhance our country's image
Serve with dedication, undaunted spirit and courage.

'Deep' Appreciation and felicitations

Respect warriors of all country's safeguarding their Nations with dedication

DEAREST DEEDU - BYE SYDNEY

We all shared most sacred art
As you touched thy motherly part.
Expressions of lovable true care
Made us lucky & day's thrill share

We adore twin little big dolls, down under
They are bright beacons for family care
Appreciate the vibrant attitudes
An Expression of acumen with aptitude

Across horizon of imaginations of lovely angels
Wonderfully deep acute cute angles
Brought sheer cheer to life unbound
Twinkles in eye, facial glow went around.

Returned with bags of memories cherished load
Cherish those passion, company aboard
Blessings flew through pure love medium
Reflected on warm memory Album

Time took us all to distant dwellings
With regards we bow, for teary parting

Deep Reciprocates

GIFT OF LIFE

Drizzle of thought droplets bring positivity
Fall slowly on mind's slide of relativity
Cause ripple effects on heart vents
With deep impacts of thought intents

Fathom soul's aspiration and expectation
Solely to appreciate creations
Navigate with compass on high tides
Guided by nature's accreditations

Embrace everyone with reverence
Share life gifts by priceless endurance
Live life to the brim to inspire
build trust with harmony's presence.

Encourage threads of unity in humanity
Guard against odds with tenacity
Realize our social commitments
And strong will to honour sentiments

Express gratitude for the gift of life
With a sense of humility tile.
Serve humanity till the last hour
Perform your role of imparting care

'Deep' smiles with gift of God

CELEBRATIONS OF LIFE

Strain to enliven other's lives
One has to run on razor balance
Provide platforms for pleasure
Give credence to moments for a glance

Close barriers to sail through adversities
That create mental stress & stains
Provide impulses of heavenly experience
Pull up pulse rates to support & sustain.

Gather soft petals with smiling gestures
Build a constant source of fragrance.
Collect others thoughts with positivity
Create deep peace relativity.

Evolve and dissolve difference of opinion
Rainbow colours emerge with fresh option.

'Deep' in thoughts life celebration

NEW YEAR RESOLUTIONS

As everyone bids good bye
To tumultuous year gone by
We invoke Almighty's blessings
Refresh our mind, by celestial offerings

Let all cherish glows on faces
Shower affectionate love places
As we all welcome New Year with Joys
Raise hopes of safe coexistence ways.

Share glimpse of smiles at every corner
Indulge in close dance on welcome runner.
Touch everyone's hearts, with soft feathers
Evolve passion to create sunshine weather.

Aspire for beginning of clean air & energy
Bring soft bright rays of tranquillity synergy.
Balance with skill on heart & mind fulcrum
Establish harmony in life chanted invocation

May universe dwell and swell in serenity
Awaken self from inner side, with divinity

'Deep' thoughts on a 'New Year' eve

LOVE BIRDS

Embark on Love port to import compassions
Your eternal voyage would be lovelorn reflections
Prayers be placed in shades of mutual concerns
Enjoy life's vestibule, fathom heart's soft veins.

Stay hand in gloves till the destination
Celebrate moments on love mission
March together in sync, with steps of trust bond
Cherish life nectar in deep filled cups of peace around

While you take off on honeymoon, on starry night
May you bring back memories of a new life's sight.
Height of togetherness, blossoms by wedding strings.
Spray happiness on mind's canopy love wings.

May you build a palace, with bricks of confidence
Surely intimacies will grow with providence.
Feel presence of eternal essence on petal's hand
As soulmates solely share closeness truly grand.

Remain drenched in deep appreciation pond
May you pass through thought's merry go round.

Deep poetic gift
For couple on wedding day

DEMOCRACY OR HYPOCRACY

Where public shivers & shrugs out of disgust
Public is mentally whipped on emoting by trust.

Power misused more often than used to trounce
Masses generally compromise, as promises bounce.

Where common sense is uncommon & peers unfair
Power impose misrule & rise on own ego tower

Petty politics cause terminal ailments of pure agony
Faith is shaken by remote torture on human anatomy.

Vanity vanishes vividly & sanity drowns in crevices
Bridges of lies are crowned by mere fallacies

Empathy is alluding, crushed under debris of hopes
Leaders fail in basic roles, play public cause.

Where share of clean air provision is at premium
Society's resource used as personal ladder platform.

Deeply undemocratic society governance across the globe

PEACE SPACE

May ever lasting peace radiate
Everywhere in ethereal spaces
May ever growing peace reign
Over world's tranquil places.

May keepers of peace flourish
Rise on trees of human assets
May sense of mental peace flow
Touch universal peace targets

May realization of co-existence
May transcend on warring zone lords.
May peace be a weapon to stop wars
Eliminate danger on humans chopped by swords.

May we perceive real for peace
Exist to glance growths & prosperity
May all receive cherished peace awards
Bright fully merge with natures propensity

"Deep" Peace space Mission

SANDWICHED MIDDLE CLASS

Looking between privileged & downtrodden
Imaginations wander through reality world garden

Eroding memories, en route forest of adversity
Realized threats, so real for poor social negativity

Looked like soft sandwich, devoid of care & concern
Fend for surviving cascading paths, by high discern.

Dilemma on faces, starved cries, alone yet aloud
Struggle to match surrounding to hear crowed crowd.

Though every heartbeat of middle classes do yearn
Remain on main poverty line with no public concern.

Meted double whips, from both front's, whisper
Walk on tight hope rays, balance needs & desire.

Deep made reality checks from all angles
Exposing middle class sandwiched by struggles.

Deep treatise

FRONT WARRIORS OF NATIONS

Look around greener side of country, really wide
Share concern over sacrifices on border entry

Selfless service, fighting for Nation's safety
Won grim battles, lost lives, bereft priority

Trying time in adversity, operate in dark terrains
Deserve empathy of National safety missions

Need true care we all feel from inside
Words of support boost their self pride

Encourage your dedication, skill's stride
Safety of lives on border's either side

Support with trust & heartfelt gratitude
Keeping all safe, feelings of deep pride

Praise missions, on separate fronts
Bow heads for life sacrifices on both ends

'Deep' admirations of front warriors

Expression of warrior's appreciation, on vital fronts of
Nation's borders.

DEEPAK SHAIL SHARE AFFECTIONS

Jointly emote expressions of love blooming
Sharing delightfully carved path strong mind

Thoughts of concern, with passion around
Together to lift expectations & strong bond

Lurking with joy mission in-bound
Life on celebrations, as smiles rebound

Move forward in life, like love doves
Carry love affair, and passion prowess

Fly high on tarmac, by wings of life's wisdom
System ready for turbulence free mission

Cherish gift of companionship on faith & trusts
Build ecstasy moments & adorn crests

Spread intimacy shower on dreamy journey of life
Union of thoughts, superb delight strides

Remain fully involved embrace value additions
Bring family unity by charming cheer creations

'Deep' celebrations on anniversary occasion

My poetic digital gift export to US from all of us

ETERNAL BLISS

Confines of oft beat heart, blessed in ovations
Tiny worldly crest flourish, with joy & aspirations

Clouds of love, built a west, by life time pleasures
Vibrating chants grow, on few pulsating ample impulse

Cascading thought waves arise, and flow
Aspirations merge in sights, on a full moon glow

Strengthens to break life's monotony
Moving on fast track, on time wheel's anatomy

Prized life's sojourn, a cash God's gift, you did sow
Deep sentiments flow instantly, steer by an arrow.

'Deep' in eternal bliss OM NAMAH SHIVAY

WOMEN EMPOWERMENT

Seeking patronage of women with trusted traits
Bow with gratitude, they deserve life time crest
Never been really easy or simple assurance
Blend and build relationship bonds of endurance

Keep firm head on neck, to align appreciations
Bring loads of affection and passion's vocations
Compassion's share brings family value addition
Firm views with dignity & pursue path of emotion

Displays virtuous ways, sacred paths of humility
Strong wheel, morale support & physical chemistry
With prideful attire, devotionally surrenders life line
Smoothens sojourn, by reassuring words for life time

Attire of sacrifice, dedication & blessings of a deity
Dwells in hearts and mind alike, as a life time duty
Balances relationship artistic equality fulcrum
Worships family culture on equal platform of quality forum

Builds beliefs, Inspiration sources & imbibes hopes
Embarking on port of love, affections by thrill scopes
Engages flawless anchoring by life's rudder stick
Ensures destiny wheels run smooth by track tricks

'Deep' empowered vision

ON WAY TO ETERNITY

Sought blessings with sights of credences
Horizon the destination's limitless places
Almighty's omnipresence on mind's inner side
Life would exist, only with prayer's from inside

Enroute wisdom zone, pure love all
Will always be in heart's veins ways
Though don't deserve life treats
God would dwell in our minds always

Choice to stay in tender hearts do remind
True essence of life & boasts to rewind
Sea of hopes would sail to wave's shores
Blissful presence brings a strong anchor

Pray for benign presence within Embrace not abandon till last breath
Grateful attainment of final salvation Transit via eternity routes for life's wealth

"Deep" Lifeways.
Prayers always on eternal peace voyage.

TOO DEEP

Life is too short, to take revenge in disguise
Make it too adorable to resist the prize
Attempt to tempt too with love's twist
Touch heart vibrations soft &safe to exist

Flow thoughts too by pleasing words
Bring harmony too for love revisit
Spread love too to win heart's strands
Walk on lanes too dark that our risky albeit

Never miss too precious heart beatings
Life span is too short to lose even a bit
Always yearn too, to earn 'His' blessings
Share a smile too, enlighten others face too

Emotions are simply too much to express Build
roots of Deep words to shoot too

Too deep rhyming attempts

POPE- THE LAST HOPE

Amid fading hope, world lost a great soul, Pope the last ray of hope
Crusader of Socialist healthy system, across as human strong rope

Merged into holy Christ left world in vacuum for sights of mourn
Departed 'Star' humanist across bay, after Sombre sojourn

Religious 'Guru' beyond praises, on adorable mission of charity
Growth in peace devotion for down trodden, a true divinity

An epitome of humility & kind soul reflect human serenity
Transits to eternal peace status, rest with the Almighty

Shock waves hurt tore humanity's tender love bond
Built by a beloved, deep faith of human sea around

"Deep" Bereaved world

TERRORISM BLOWS

Mind wanders on wild psyche of Mass destructions
Blasting moments & ill intentions wish cause turmoil
Fear on helpless faces wipe off few generations
Smash ear drums & peace hope pieces to land on soil

Thoughts wonder, to whip way laid terror filled minds
Aspired to weaken roots of peace carts
Attempt to shatter hopes, few ones left behind
Disgrace to human race rip off hearts, lying in parts

Life slowly dragged to banks of fading lights
Fear awaited fresh attacks, on tender eye pupils
Muted witnesses face cruelty of burning rites
Silenced kins trapped by manic missionary evils.

Terror casts tragic blow, apathy on human kind
Sprinkle salt on deep wounds cause trauma on mind
Erase lifeline devoid of sympathy aroma
Crush innocents never to come out of deep Coma

Made them easy prey, by horrible dark ill designs
Rewind of cold-blooded murder alas in public view
Burial underground, life's existence on parting signs
Condole on obituary register page, for next one due

Deep remorse, condemn global terrorism

LIFE - A PHILOSOPHICAL PURSUIT

Gazing thru window moving on thought wave's train
Sandwiched human sardines, boarded crowded train
Oblivious of destiny ways, literally unknown entrain
Aging out of life's crazy ways, to different locations

Train load of thoughts detrained

Echoes of distinct calls emerged on tracks of time
Endured desperate sighs, on life's parallel rail line
Views of an eternal urge, sought visions of goals
Everyone explores life ways elude their true roles

Mirage literally so hard to explore.

Signs of impatience catch up alluring transactions
Besieged hopes & despair en route transit stations
Slowly crossed love tunnels, barriers of old patterns
Endorse all moves on ways to inner self realization

Transit of moving faces and places pulled passengers

Attempt to gain defined roles, on board deep sojourn
Noticed search lights, divine destiny's power vision

Deep black holes in the nucleolus of destiny

LIFE TIME MISSION

Life time mission, is their vision
Oh lord, its surely rare in real life
Admiration flows for those few
Who truly live life & truly strife

Nation's pride and honour are lively flying gems
Bring sparkle, through brightness from within

Wanders in sky, smooth flier on dreamy lanes
Cherishes to relive, flash back on efforts to remain

One feels vibrations take over the command
Over hearts kingdom, nostalgic memories so grand

Life time pictures emerge on gentle canvas of mind
Like sweet dreams of ferry flight, on its sturdy rewind

"Deep" Safety rewards

"GARB-DEN" CITY

While dwelling in this city
If you wander a while
You gather views, so dirty

Inhaling smoke to lungs capacity
To find your image, defaced
While dwelling in this City

Decibels of loud horns, so noisy
Stand on stops & garbage pile
You gather views, so dirty

Dust obscures faces, earlier pretty
With dusted blunder file
While dwelling in this City

Darkness often engulfs full of pity
Push dreams away a mile
You gather views, so dirty

Dirty water on roads so mucky
Chose to lose your smile treaty
While dwelling in this city
You gather views, so dirty

Deep Citation- A **Villanelle**

THOUGHT LINE

Deep thought pulled mind search engine, with wing
Fulfil ambition mission upgrade life style planning

Touch fibers of heart vibrations and reverberations
Bliss of humble efforts, to emote true online visions.

Tender thoughts blurred visions shake the life proof
On rainy nights catch thought droplets on mind roof

Taking everyone out of deep slumber comfort zones
Prayed for purity of conscience flow on divine ozone

Seek support to move away from confines of homes
Couplets emerge within as thought defines domains.

Deep in thought lines

SILENT TRANSITON

Seek His blessings, intense credence

Horizon is the ultimate limit
Of your omnipresent sight
Life without your blissful light
Has really no value or delight

Enroute, love or hate me, both are in my favor

If you love me
Will be in your heart ways
If you hate me
Will be in your mind always

Choice to dwell, within deep heart or mind

You are life's true essence
Silky smooth sail to life ashore
Live on canopy of hopes
Your soft presence, strong anchor

Seek smiles, till the last breath
You either love me or hate me

'Deep' reverenced transition

WISDOM IN ACTION

Feelings are true, reflection of expressions too
Life has been so kind, to have true friend like you
Feeling of soft touch, as the two heart resonates
Care is moving on way, to stare at the beat rates

Life will surely spring merely with hope sight
Charm of compassion would certainly delight
Let those promise of being in thoughts, kept alive
As a source of pleasures would go up & not dive

Need to control heart emotions, not overtake
Give real feel, as a friendly gift one can take
That faith never betrayes by time & priority
No one affords to share hard earned loyalty

Deep firm on mental plane with wisdom

DEEP SALUTES: ALL MOTHERS

We all await soft touch of love and flow, binds forever
Now a distant glow, as life cannot be same without her

As we attempt to regain affections missed, we endow
Regards from heart that echoes with deep sorrow

For a life time devotion, touch your feet and bow
Pray for rebirth in same format, seed to grow

Another chance together in double row here
Adore your care & seek blessings, so very dear
Away you are, but every day brings us so very near

Dear mother, we remember you always

"Deep" reverence

THOUGHT HORIZON

Sky is really torn across you two
On happy anniversary of you two
Down under chants of sacred vows

Amongst hazy **STARS** across the horizon
Twinkling around & await to descend from **SKY**
Cherished presents and appear to represent

Along with **MOON** awaiting full exploration
Love bugs being bugged on the halfway
Parting away with lost look, being compliant

Approach SUN to foster warmth & hot emission
Living united with dignity, without being slimy
Only to accept destiny ways, really dare

Under shelter serenity sowed in unison
Wish celebrations on **EARTH,** spin mission
Day to feel virtual reality & guide the planet

Horizon triangle shows **RAINBOW** glows
Deep emerges & reflects son Milky way rows

Silky Deep thought horizon

A PERFECT PROFILE

They too possess profiles, gifts of life
Granted by mother's pride- with strife

Mission venture of aspiring to Unite
Wander in nature adventure, nurture lights

Exist under fragile lease of faith line
Contended to inherite moments to sublime.

Rebuild coexistence way's foundation
Enjoy voyage destined mutual admiration

Passage without barriers to move forward.
Involve, be instrumental for love to spread

Deep strives to extend helping hands
Overcome an impasse for mission's blend

Deep voyage profound introspection

WORLD OF WORD PLAY

Not my prosaic traits, that do define me
No hooray makes a call to chasten me.

Neither aim drudgery, pique for word play.
Nor delinquent attempt for word spiral tray

My expressions cajole, few funny ones
May be labelled as nerd but amuse too

Garnet hey of hopes, seek no mediator
Enjoy world serene chirp sound of creator.

Rescind mendacious attempts of few carriers
Feigning faith in Him just to cross the barriers

Deep word play

RIOTS OF COLORFUL IMAGINATIONS

Riots of colours cast imagery of rainbow verticals
Droplets of vibrant flows spreads in seven circles.

Petals on soil play a game of colour overflow
Solar winds change garden laws, to thrust hallows

Settle down on shields of shades in the park
Anatomy of plants yield as sun rays sparks.

Analogy of gardener left trails of flower buds
Grow under an umbrella of transient clouds

Gratitude for creator we bow for colourful show
Relish bonds to nourish true love root & grow.

Under ambit of deep imaginations mood emerges
Share riots of colours strike eye sight & merges

*Deep Imagery

RAINBOW OF LIFE SHOW

Invigorate, self encourage emotions yearning
Touch pedestal of life, with natural surrounding
Challenge cross hurdles, march with adventures
Sirens of destiny tunes, invade the life apertures

Crowd attempts to starve life support of nature
Emerged out of woods, divine bliss dwelling shelter
Curing spirituality path for salvation service counters
Express desires for solutions to building new empires

Regain colour growths by leaps & bounds
Pray for existence on moments on time tested grounds
Enjoy hobby with ecstasy on genes of poetic activity
Express obligations for deep imaginations of creativity

Deep lights life show, on horizon's rainbow

VIRTUAL REALITIES

Holding a Mirror in front of your face
If you don't find reflection of double image
Without making the real image dim
If one can look straight at actual 'him'
You deserve a grace and flight

With candid frankness & clarity in your heart
If you possess creative mind & balancing art
Judge yourself, in your own eyes by being fair
Pass decree, against wrong doings with dare
You would pulsate hopes really bright.

Without any tremor or shiver in your feet
Can you stand done, against a wrong feat
Inspire faith to preserve prestige and rights
Remain unnerved, left behind alone in nights.
You would stand out in limelight.

Without any fear or favour in your heart &be kind
Can you lend an ear to lone person, get entwined
Enthuse true compassion, offer gratitude of sight
Surpass passion, be a guide and source of light
You would emerge 'Deep' from insight.

Virtually real 'Deep'

A HISTORICAL SATIRE

Try to look at human race which they have vanished
without any trace

History of empires which were destroyed & trashed to
Ashes in the past, in total disgrace

Kings outlived sporadic power innings which got lost
with turn of time to get buried in ruined palaces

Preachers of immortality who lost enroute sermon's
mission in solitudes of high hill places

Enlightened world wisdom who remain silent to be
above board without egoistic attitude, to soar free
mind sky spaces

Deep simile remains grounded as you attempt to fly
high

PHILOSOPHY OF LIFE JOURNEY

Exploring a Journey loaded with thoughts
Start emerging from a serene outpost
Built a maze of merging sea waves rides
and propelled by gravitational force tides

Castle of Deep inspiration of a young mind
Compelled emotional stock, as memories rewind
Survival in tricky world with journey destined
play a fair game with sports person in kind

Shed & shred all worldly desires
Salvation within window blinds
Grateful to the Master life memento
Worship the creator with invocation in mind

Agnideep creativity walks on flowery paths
For essence & proactive presence behind
Gazing in starry rights with cool moon shadow
Recall memorable moments, remotely entwined

Visualize His subtle presence and realize
Alive in you, as ever since soul never dies

Philosophically 'Deep'

MARCHING SENTIMENTS

Sentiments march straight from the heart
Love bonds stood test of time, from start
Spray gratitude within & soul's sole part
Silent tears swell & sail in eye care port

Stand by someone, hold him from falling apart
Lost dream load, as deep slumber starts
Body sublimates in mother earth deep parts
Pious soul leave for eternal journey restart

Shall remain in mind & everyone's heart
On distant screens of horizon, colourful art

'Deep' Sojourn

PIOUS JOURNEY

Born as a saint, a living angel Dwelling
within, as an incarnation
Eye pupils reflect devotion for the poor Shelters
sourced for downtrodden

An epitome of trust, love & compassion
Created sacred building foundation
With an adorable virtuous humility attire
Ornament of simplicity possession

Pious journey of heavenly existence
Served selflessly, with fair execution
Age or physical condition, of no consequence
Never carved for people's adoration

Countrymen bow in adoration
Unflinching spirit of sophistication
Trust investment on humanity
Reflect growth of love accumulation

Deep Voyage

SO WHAT, AFTER THAT

May script number of couplets on inner beauty
If wrinkles appear on faces, then what after that?

Strong stature may gain straight success
If spine bends its shape, then what after that?

If bee kisses all flower in rosy garden
If time dries its essence, then what after that?

If thoughts snatch juicy fruits, plucking around
If words fail to stop them, then what after that?

One could roam with love for sky treasure hunt
If one has no flight of thoughts, then what after that?

One could attempt to honour sentiments glow
If light can't stop darkness, then what after that?

Deep Questions but nobody answers so what, after that?

Deep Inquisitiveness

UNEXPRESSED SENTIMENTS

Explored obscure unshared feelings
Removed internal ignorance of many
Raised their dampened lost spirits
With flowers stored sweet honey

Created magical moments of life energy
With glances of charming company
Enlightened every heart with synergy
With options to compose harmony

Left no stones unturned in the world
Mitigated everyone's agony word
Words are not the only medium
Reflected mind by poetic symphony

Eyes too played vital part to convey
Facial expressions provided testimony
Lip movements carried heart's sensation
Prayed silently to reach human destiny

Deep Express Ways unexpressed

DEEP TRANSITION

Transiting with eternal attire
Moving towards blue oblivion
Hopeful creations will embark
On mind ships of future generation

Take a pleasant nip & slip to oblivion
Deep slumber mode turns into a champion
Pay my final salutes to life by invocation
Surely, will be safe on final transition

Invigorate meaning of word existence
Mull over tall stacks of public opinion
Expression of gratitude emerges on horizon
Like earth revolving around sun like an icon

Sail on cruise with multitude option vision
Arrive with pious soul, on sole destination
Yearn to earn repetition of current sojourn
With blessing of enshrined God in heaven

Deep in Transition mode

LIFE TIME CELEBRATIONS

Honour prideful glorious “Hours”
Embrace graceful year’s “Minutes”
Serve humanity on fleeting “Seconds”

Strive earnestly to slow shower care
Bring hearty smiles on fellow travellers
Care love human beings with pleasure.

Face agonizing patterns of celestial journey
Encourage family traditions & Value harmony
Shower affection petals, as part of love testimony

Strengthen will power, contribute to family bonds
Remain contended alike & share love unbound
Display compassion & true spirit of trust around

On your special day of celebrations of life.
Our true prayers for Joys with no strife

Cross the milestone with prideful association
Remain blessed with family & enjoy relaxation

Agni Deep celebrates Life

LIFE CORALS

Elimination by lustrous moon shine spree
Emerging autumn blue sky, across pine tree
Waves radiate to create natural mood swing
Remain afloat with fighter flying challenge wing

Adorn garland from land of beauty
Lotus of world blooms in thoughts
Effulgent faith of multitudes traits
Beatitude in reverence, we sought

Verily divine form of graceful embodiment
Express gestures of ambient energy pool
Celebrations of triumph & life's merriment
Anointed, to bestow wisdom thru whirlpool

Ornament of Red vermillion on foreheads
Dazzles the worshipper by hopes beads Attain
celestial vibration with positive vibes
Keeps eternal bond on drive by trust thread

Carve scriptures of Almighty's reflections
Glance resonance of voyage unifications
Encompass to meet gravity challenges
Only to admire his trusted deep creations.
"Deep" Gratitude

SOBRE MEMORY SHADOWS

One sat quietly in sombre mood
On passing off of life partner
Face parting pain for life
Hurting and thought's loneliness

Eternal bow of marital union fire
Turned blow of rising Pyre by air
Heart & mind on slow reconciliatory moods
Turmoil cause upheaval on life roads

His appeal to fill grief of life pits
Would remain an eye sore on teary eyelid
Deep inside, remorse grew everyday
Accept facts of life and destiny way

Reminiscences of golden memory album
Moments of care & share sire
Reflect on thought horizon so often
Ecstasy feelings always gather

Blue-sky screen reflected on collage
Build hope drain, flow out mental cage
Yet can't find viable for life to engress
Face no option situation for entire race

Deep hopes of reunion of lifetime partner

JOURNEY OF TOGETHERNESS

Grand oval sun-rise
        Shines on corner left window

Blessings of almighty arise
        Surf & troll from right window

Closeness spreads aroma
        Flying above cloud nine horizon

Transit in few seconds into space
        Divinity of company raises spirit

Prayers cross sound barrier decibel
        Bring peace of mind to Life & enable

Feel blessed by almighty, as ever
        Ever ready to move away forever

Deep togetherness

CROSS ACROSS THE HORIZON

On shockingly passing away
So suddenly & too far away

Shock waves caused distress rounds
Fear of being left ajar, hurt all around

Hard to imagine isolated life without a ship
Missed forever, your grand companionship

An iron-willed person, fought health adversities
Pillar of family & friends to imbibe royal qualities

Built an aura by presence with a difference
Charms of personality deserves reverence

Deserve our deep respects in ovation
Salute profile in person with invocation

Deep expressions on loss of a respected person

FLOW SOULFUL FLOW

Flow my soul flow, on compassion's sole
As till the end, one would never know
Alarm of last breath, would give silent blow

So spread cheers on surface, bring out of shadow
Move with gratitude on soul's distinct glow
Pray for empathy by humanity to steadily grow

Bid good bye to materialistic world sorrows
Nature evolves to enrich, by rays of sharp edge arrows
Leave past behind & grow love roots deep below

Soulful flow out of herd like fleeting sparrows
Converge to serve priceless ecstasy & endows
Visualize & utilize every moment silent flows

March of time from present to future is never slow
Enjoy what is in your plate invoke to bow before
Invoke & practice love, as sign off world show

Deep soul flow

FRESH DEEP CREATION

Lights of drying lamp, extinction by air is moral story
Winds are cursed to revenge without a glory

Plans remain alive, yet appear inconclusive
Avoid day dreams, since can't be inclusive

Few attempts to enlighten life lamp of hearts
But careless & ruthless don't share even tiny part

Remain elated to survive dark passage always
Like kites be experts to fly in winds upper ways

Deep conclusions

DEEP BLESSINGS

Priceless gift of God, lucky sights of an angel.
Blissful emotion grew delightful angle
Cherish outcome of mental stress strained
Your home blessed by cheerful little doll engrained

Proudly envisage & enjoy conversion of dream
Power of prayer brought glory for parent team
Feel & fathom charms of new role & thrills inside
Boosted the status from couple to parent's pride

Feel tiny feet move with rhythm of offspring
Capture pleasure sight, to bind by memory's string
Enjoy moment of love creation by a bundle of joy
Pinnacle of family happiness, showered lovely toy

Share smiles along with Eklavya rhyme
Capture little foot prints on sands of time

Deep ecstasy moments for our family

AGNI'S AGONY

Imagine someone in deep agony
Faced tricky ways of dark destiny
Herculean task, never been tiny

Unravelled universe's elusive mystery
Perceive his charms and chemistry
Achieved milestone of Journey history

Travelled on thorny ways so hazy
Climbed on hope ladder to risky
Focussed on aim & marched steady

Cross barriers of trust deficit iron
Jump deep pits& cascading journey
Built foundation of faith in harmony

Woke up before reaching dark destiny
Examined life, is true testimony
Resolved not to preach but end agni's agony.

Deep in Agony

MISSING YOU

Sharing sordid moments of parting
Soft blissful presence now evading
Movement of thoughts on heart's mutiny
Our sojourn together, fell apart by destiny

Eyes sour & hurt, on leaving out of sight
Fleeting glow, trailing vision, trilling outright
Disturbed by final shift of life time anchor on ground
Trusted hands merged on distant sea shore around

Serenity of innocent smile rode on sad sailing waves
Rhythm of humming sounds mentally raves
Aura of priceless existence heart grateful mind
Lost amidst memories of a lifelong friend

Yearn for those flowing arms, hope not in futility
As eternal affections, wishes descend & dreams to fructify

Yearn Deep blessings

GIFT OF FIVE SENSES

Looking through sand hour glass
Lying ajar, at a distance on atlas
Gift of five senses showered on mind
Expressed ways, to communicate in kind

Heart echoes in thought's deep valleys
For brief rest in Nature resort trolleys
Nostrils trilled by extra strong fragrance
With deep inhalation of pure essence

Tasted cuisines of Nature's menu
Sitting across distant Sky fence venue
Felt passionate & deep sense showers
For wisdom droplets, live from happy towers

Thoughts flow on blue canvas up to core
Casted rainbow sight, with riots of colours

Transit to trans state by imagining
Gift of five senses blessed on human being

Deep gift senses

NUPITAL THOUGHTS

Under the blue-sky hazy contour sights
Brew romance in dim street lights

Emerged memories of seven round vows
Start merging with starry night rows

Twinkling eyes shined with broad smiles
Mirrored reflection of lovely dreams

Whispering woods in thought jungle
Mingled in unison of slow body sublime

Wander in wonderland remaining together
Ride on emotional hightides really higher

Life partner's sojourn, travel till eternity
Blessings from top, showers nectar affinity

Nuptial night's Deep imagination

REAL TIGER

Human ocean gathered with Tear
On passing away of their real tiger
Built apolitical stage of coloured flower
To pay homage and tribute's shower

As pyre engulfed to realms of destiny
Crowd assembled from all community
Was an uncrowned king of millions
Built people's hopes and aspirations

Choked emotions visible for pious soul
Transiting to other side of fence & stroll
Love of masses, Bala Saheb, their leader
Now moving on cart of tear wheel stair

Deep merger in Panch. Tatva final Salvation
human sight, endless plight, stand in ovation

Deep Tiger of Mumbai Maharashtra

SEACRUISE WANDERFUL JOURNEY

Rising sun grew steadily on snow clad mountains
Nascent soft rays built the day with fast momentum
Multitudes of colourful coral emerged through life prisms
Shadows shifted swiftly from snow subsiding patterns

Serenity of nature raised spirits of troop voyagers
Fleeting sight of whale's high jump for on lookers
Joyous group turned as a family on vacation
Starry fraternity mixed around, strong bond aspiration

Nature's precious gift of heavenly creations
Made sojourn of life time closeness reasons
Memories of fairy sea cruise our maiden experience
Built dreamy affairs, felt sustained family presence

'Deep' Experience of fantasy world

On board cruise, trip to ten European countries as a group tour

HER MAJESTY

It has never been straight or simple play
To seek woman's empathy & empowered way
One needs to face displeasure sometimes
Bowing down never, to men's unfair crimes

Realize blending efforts, building bonds
With loads of pure affections all around
Appreciate strong stand, not to appease
Neither nods head to align for towing boss

Disallows exploitation opportunity or chance to stay
Nor attaches values to uncultured ways
Indulges never on issues if irrelevant
Avoids risky brawls of deceit trends

Wins attention by sights of self enlightenment
On wheels of moral strength & true talent
Never aspires for changing ideas or attributes
Strengthens confidence & pays only tributes

Pinpoints own shortcomings with deep courage
Minces no words to support on dark patches
Witness proficient handling of home chores
On shore of turbulence, touches own tough cores

Deep praises

FRIENDSHIP PEARLS

Life has blessed me friend like you
Resonate heart echo, emotionally true

Built by bricks of friendship cemented in mind
Thoughts of cycling down to college do remind

Passion crossed barriers of study curriculum
Bonds of affection, created lifelong support fulcrum

Remained anchored in life, with deep harmony
On tryst of destiny ways, without an iota of agony

Always remained close to heart as in thoughts
Boosted morale in admiration of friendship of sports.

Deep remembrances of college days to shoot fast moving Electrons with Protons & Neutrons parked in the pearl's nucleus of an Atomic friendship dear friend.

NATURE'S DROPLETS

Drizzle droplets flow steadily & land
Drips on mind, to ripple deep impacts
Heart beats create rhythm, really grand
Fathom soul's aspirational effects

Adorable creations of wonderful nature
Blissful screen shots of eternity nurture
Navigate, as remote guide eco system
Eliminate darkness & enlighten "His" stream

Imbibe precious life time rare treasures
Enhance love, in mother nature's honour
Share lurking hopes on heart's pleasure
Happy hours mixed with value addition share

Endorse praiseworthy colourful cart
Reflect true smiles & purity of heart
Create mirror image as gratitude start
Enlarge insights of connoisseur's part

Deep accolades on Nature's Droplets

YAAS DISASTER

Yilting under scary tidal waves whips
Cascading whirlpools cause rise of ships
Impending glooms create chaotic shores
Gushing winds blow floating light house stores

Safety from sordid “Yaas” cyclonic disaster
As high sea tides play a roller coaster
Dampened spirits of distressed masses
Under deep impact on coastal places

Sights of nature’s might & human helplessness
Surf for traces of life in be wilderness
Protect precious patience and perceive Yaas play
Sea of a difference mirage display

Mitigate misery, mission to merge merriment
Aboard rough & tough wave movements
Nature’s ways to display coral reefs
As barriers drowned under public relief

Deep drowns in sights across the coastal lines

THE WORLD IS YOURS TOO

Having boarded the thought train loaded like sardines
Changing view's backdrop bring images of past times

Stepping on soul track distraught by suffocations
Realized shortness of life journey stress & strains

Crossed emotional tunnels of darkness merged mind
Similar to ignorance casting shadows on left behind

Running over bridges to narrow side & allied
Upper chamber in slumber, fragility of body ride

Attempt & be calm & firm to hold destiny ways
Avoid being derailed on parallel tracks always

To fathom the aim of living as a human being
Soul's on constant change of attire & transiting

Worldly Deep

HOLDING THE POETIC ROSES

Unfair possessiveness of prose paragraphs
Fair validation of poetry rays heart graphs

Poems always held in high esteem by teams
Couplets impact to strike bull point with beams

Adopt better softer routes for inner expression
Transmit thoughts from heart to mind as passion

Pen is mightier than knife keep it flowing
Win a heart not hurt a mind by blowing

Rise to higher pedestal, cross word impasses
Let creations get treasured status in places

Poetical Deep hold

CATASTROPHIC POLITICAL WAVES

Apathy of jarring political subversions
Indulge in blame game with distortions
Witness cruel brick bats of extreme invasions
Bureaucracy engulfs democracy in utter violations

Bild parties on broken foundation by villains
Morally corrupt yet white attired in desperations
Owners of power platforms unite to divide the nation

A Gatha of politicians harming new generation

Deeply catastrophic tricks of poly-ticks

MY SALUTES SIR

We always yearned to earn
Your affections and care forever
Building an eternal bond
You laid foundation of true-life share

An unsurmountable feeling of loss
On professional doyen's departure
Deep bids tearful tributes
As emotions play havoc on mind aperture

Voyage of parting sentiments
Lead us to past memory albums
Shocking news of final navigation
Mood us to life fulcrum

Shower immense devotions for cheerful 'Romil' treat
Reflection of ideal companion under "madan" ambit

Final Deep salutes

DEEP VOWS

We all await touch of love flow bonds
Forever form a distant glow
Isolated life lost with a sorrow
We miss your shelter and shadow

Heartful regards echo in minds valley
Bow and cherish devotion on accounts tallied
Pray for re birth in same family
Seek providence to be together & ally

Adorable care Adorned blessings now missing
Away you have gone, everyday we are remembering

Deep vows

CHERISHED RESPONSES

Dear Agni

Heartiest congratulations.

You have used your time remarkably well, in multifarious activities. May God Bless you & your creativity aspirations.

Late Air Marshal ML Sethi PVSM, AVSM.

Dear Agnihotri

The composition of your poems on various aspects of life, truly reflect your poetic visions and are praiseworthy. I am sure, the average reader will find these Poems interesting & thought provoking.

It gives me immense pleasure to find a veteran excelling in various fields, which enhances the appeal of the Armed forces. I take this opportunity to wish greater success to your poetic endeavors in future.

Air Chief Marshal. FH Major PVSM, AVSM, VSM, VM.

Creative writing is an Art which derives fruitful purpose and results from fertility of mind & intensity of expressions with 'Deep' impact on each & every persons thought process. Poetry is one such creative medium of expression & creative writing skills.

The author has certainly a flair for writing, which is praise worthy. His poems are regularly published in various magazines & journals including the 'AFWWA' Annual magazine "SANGINI".

My best wishes for your creative ventures & future "Poetic Expressions".

Mrs. Harveen Krishnaswamy.
Former President "Air Force Wives Welfare Association" – On release of second Book "Deep Reflections".

Dear PK
I admire your creative ability to write Poetry & Prose. Nice reflections of your spontaneous Deep Expressions. I enjoyed and could not stop reading your poem till I reached the end. GOD has bestowed you with brilliant Poetic skills. God Bless you for your efforts. Best of Luck

Maj Gen (DR) S Venkatraman (Retd) Former President, AFNOE Dwarka.

Your Poetry is indeed "Touching"
Lt Gen Gurmeet Singh, PVSM, VYSM, AVSM, VSM (Retd)
Former Dy Chief of Army Staff
Present Governor, Uttarakhand

Dearest Deepu,

I really don't seem to keep up with your literary skills & achievements. That does not mean, I lack appreciations for then. I am eagerly waiting for release of your third Poetry collection release. All the best of wishes for future poetic endeavors.

So proud of you. I remember reading most of them with tearful eyes, due to expressions of compassions. You are so spontaneous. Enjoyable
great writing.
Well done

Dr Priti Pandey Sister Sydney Mr. K S Pandey & family.

My Dear Deepu

"Yun mere zehan me alfaz kam pad gaye
Tere jajbaton, khayalon ki tareef ke liye"

I truly admire your creative skills & vision on life angles, emotions &romance with varied expressions, observations are exemplary. Beauty of right usage of words, originality of thoughts brings freshness with a difference. Touch everyone's hearts and emotions, matching realities of life, to soar in the sky and beyond. Creations cast deep impacts by the power of language & poetic skills. A way of your attaining spirituality through this medium of emoting. May God give strength, to create an enviable place in Poetry world with blessings& best wishes

Meena Agnihotri Life time Sangini

Wah, Kya Baat Hai! Dear Bhai

Yes, that's my spot appreciation, for your instant response through your couplet, on sharing my few lines. Quite realistic, deeply interesting & motivating to core of our heart.

Dr Prashant Agnihotri M.S., MNAMS, FICO, Founder– Retina Care Hospital, Nagpur Dr Ms Jaishree and family.

It is a matter of great happiness that Group Captain Pradeep Agnihotri is publishing his third Poetry collection. As the rays of light of Sun spreads in all directions, his poems on Social & Current subjects created in distinctive styles would impact everyone. We are sure, appreciations & encouragements from the readers will flow as in his precious two publications. On behalf of 'Agnihotri' family, we wish him success in the current Publication.

Mr. Prabhat Agnihotri, Director 'Tech-Expert' consortium ltd Pune, Mrs Neelam Agnihotri and family

---

Dear Bhai Saheb

Poetry helps to understand & appreciate the world around. It gives rhythm of silence, light to darkness & magic of metaphor, compactness of expressions, use of five senses, besides simplicity of meaning in few lines. All the Best

Er Rajive, Leena Bajpai and family, Bangluru.
Co-brother & Sister-in-law

Respected Jijaji

Great & Proud moments for all of us. Poetic lines of few of your poems straight from the heart are so true

“Our life can never exist without prayers”
“Faith enlighten us, in our deep sojourn”

Simply a masterpiece with beautifully crafted expressions. Tears started rolling down. Unable to express feelings of gratitude in words. Very beautiful creations crafted by talented hands. Overwhelmed by all the love & affections, Respectful regards

Er Deepak- Shailja Shukla and family USA
Brother in-Law & graceful sister in Law

A very touching description of the imagined flow of life, in the composition ‘Shared Will’. Especially in advancing years. Fear of uncertainties, expected worries and emerging emotions, very well depicted. True reflections of stark reality of life.... as in the end, nobody knows when, where & how your realty of assets ‘WILL’ be perceived Cherish every moment now, not tomorrow, as it will never be the same, to truly enjoy your creations & images built.

Mrs Pushpa & Gp Capt (Dr) R K Shrivastav VSM.

A rendition springing out from the core of one's heart. It cannot be commented by anyone's mind sunk in the world with worldly thoughts.

Air Commodore S H Tripathi AVSM Former JAG (Air)

Excellent piece of your writing skins – very apt for majority of the cases. Very touching for those having similar sentiments but can't express. Very well scripted.

Wing Commander DS Virdi An IAF colleague

Extremely well written Sir, Congratulation. You are better off than many of us, who do not have those possessions as 'creations' or 'Creative Expressions in such affluent & luxurious emotional world of words. That is the legacy that makes your 'will'. So proud of you sir. Best wishes are always there & are compounded every day.

A serving IAF colleague

It is wonderful. You have poured your heart in to Poetry Sir. All the Best.

A Serving Colleague of IAF

Dear Pradeep

Wish you pen an autobiography, after your third book publication. It will be an interesting read. It will certainly inspire everyone and boost our morale besides a pride of Serving & Retired Defense personnel. You have gained exemplary exposure in poetry writing field, as a literary artist in the world of words.

With your meteoric rise from a student of Science & Electronics during postgraduation to achieve glory in the IAF sojourn, as logistician and later exposure in the Corporate world. It has been an adorable journey, to touch an enviable status as a poet.

ESM Mr. R S Rai Ex IAF, extended family member.

Dear Pradeep

You have been sharing so many poems in the past. I am really at a loss to express on each of your lovely creations. I feel your poems are very touching to the heart. I find that poet is in love with his creativity.

ESM Mr. Suhas Ingle Ex IAF